9 Things that Drive Measurable Patient Volume

Driving the Right Patient, with the Right Payer, to the Right Service Line

9 Things that Drive Measurable Patient Volume

Driving the Right Patient, with the Right Payer, to the Right Service Line

By John Luginbill

ISBN 978-1-105-62780-4

Contents

Foreword by Stewart Schaffer

In his book, *9 Things That Drive Measurable Patient Volume*, John Luginbill provides the healthcare industry C-suite and marketing professionals with an invaluable road map for controlling their own new patient development and market share destiny. His insights, tactics and strategies are as clear a marketing dissertation as I have ever read on what is a very complex subject. Behind each of his 9 recommendations stands years of multi-industry marketing experience, up-to-date best practices, and a style of communication that is disarmingly clear and straightforward.

The simplicity of John's recommendations is at the center of his brilliance. Most marketing mavens would have taken this same subject matter and expanded it into a much longer and more complicated book. However, John's approach eliminates all of the background noise that is out there and gets right to the core of our healthcare marketing challenges. Anyone in healthcare marketing today would be extremely well served to develop a plan that implements the 9 things John says will drive measurable patient volume. I am quite confident that those who overlook or ignore John's strategies will in the near future be losing significant market share to those who aggressively take his advice.

Stewart Schaffer
Chief Marketing and Strategy Officer
BayCare Health System
Clearwater, Florida

Introduction

Introduction to the Second Edition

In 2009, I wrote the first edition of this book. I say I wrote it, but it was more like I compiled it in a few days from some posts I made on my blog and some speeches I was giving at the time. It was meant to summarize my opinions about hospital and medical practice marketing: 1) if you don't find a way to drive bottom line contribution margin (also know as profit), then you are just useless overhead, and 2) marketing done right can actually improve outcomes and contribute to clinical excellence.

The book was available for download on my blog, TurnUpYourVolume.com; on my agency's site, TheHeavyweights.com; and on Kindle. Surprisingly, people downloaded it thousands of times. So I reread it to see what value they were seeing in the book. While there were some good nuggets of healthcare marketing wisdom, it was largely an incoherent mess and almost impossible for anyone but the most dedicated reader to finish. I had one reader tell me that if he was a hostage deep in the jungles of South America and my book was the only thing he had to read, he would give up reading. Not exactly a shining endorsement, but people just kept downloading it anyway.

So this is my shot at redemption. I have cleaned up this book a bit: it still won't be great reading, but at least it's a lot more readable now. It should also be a lot more accessible to people new to healthcare marketing, without so much of the insider jargon used exclusively in healthcare.

Oh, and if you know one of those poor souls that paid for a Kindle copy of the first edition, have them call or email me and I'll give them a copy of this second edition for free as an apology.

John P. Luginbill
March 2012

Preface

Hospital marketing is unique in the marketing world. Very few people know how to actually drive business into a hospital. I am trying to change that.

If you are a healthcare marketer, your job is to drive the right patient, with the right payer, into the right DRG or CPT. Why? Because if you do your job right, you will actually save lives, lower the cost of clinical service delivery, and increase the financial sustainability of your organization.

Read that last sentence again. Healthcare marketing done right can do all that: bring in money, lower costs, and save lives. Yes, *all that*. How? By using marketing methodologies like segmentation to target those who are actually in need of health care, then driving them to where they can get help.

Accountable Care Organizations (ACOs) began to operate nationwide as of January 2012. The whole point of the Medicare Shared Savings Program is to reduce healthcare costs, cut inefficient resource allocation, and improve patient care. Whether or not you work in an ACO, every provider will be expected to get those exact same improvements.

This is not just a clinical challenge: there is also a lesson here for healthcare marketers. If you are not showing ways to reduce healthcare costs, stop inefficient resource allocation (e.g., wasting money on useless marketing), or improve patient care, then you are just an unnecessary expense and an endangered species in the health system.

Good news! Marketing can reduce healthcare costs by targeting patients who have a high probability of needing medical care.

Marketing resources are used efficiently when you segment the market, measure and revise to maximize results, and then spend your marketing resources to target only DRGs/CPTs in the three-way intersection where your expertise, capacity, and contribution margin all meet. A common mistake is to assume that all the marketing "best practices" that work for other types of products will also work for healthcare providers. This can be an unfortunate waste of time, money, and resources.

Healthcare marketing is idiosyncratic. There's nothing else exactly like it. You can't sell it with branding like a bottle of Coke, or drive traffic to your locations with promotions like McDonald's. There is no shopping experience with price/quality comparisons. Nobody, including you, knows what it actually costs to get a procedure done in your facility. The person who uses the service doesn't actually pay for it: a third-party insurance company or the government negotiates the price and pays the bill. Cost is not an issue, quality is hard to determine, promotion is against federal law, and branding does not work. Name another product with that set of marketing challenges—*it doesn't exist.*

My agency team and I have worked with some of America's greatest brands, such as Thomas' English Muffins, Nike, McDonald's, Walmart, and Procter & Gamble. Those opportunities have taught us that many of the strategies that are effective in selling consumer brands cannot be directly applied to healthcare.

Knowing this fuels my passion to reach out to healthcare marketers. I know that when I provide the right help and advice, that knowledge helps healthcare marketers participate in saving patients' lives. That's what makes our job meaningful.

However, just like consumer marketing, healthcare marketing should demonstrate measurable Return on Investment (ROI). If you aren't doing that as a marketer, you are just unnecessary overhead to the system—and if your department hasn't already been slashed, it will be soon.

So why do I want to change health system, clinic, and physician group marketing? Because it is important to America and to the communities that providers serve. Very few of the necessary services that health systems, clinics, or physician groups provide their community make money on the bottom line, so marketers must support financial sustainability by driving the things that *do* make money.

Providing healthcare services to your community is a holy mission—a healing and lifesaving mission. Marketing has not traditionally been considered a higher calling, but in the case of healthcare, marketing has a critical role to play in delivering the mission of saving lives and healing. It starts by using segmentation and targeting to identify those in need of healthcare and leads to financial sustainability that keeps the doors open.

My hope is that you will choose to read the next nine chapters, describing nine proven things you can start right away to drive money into your provider organization, and begin the journey to understanding how healthcare marketing contributes to the *holy mission.*

You can read more of my thoughts on hospital marketing at TurnUpYourVolume.com or follow me on Twitter at @JohnLuginbill.

MEASURABLE PATIENT VOLUME

Step #1

TARGET A SPECIFIC PATIENT

A health system CEO once told me, "Bring the right patient, with the right payer, to the right service line." Let's break down that statement into three parts: *right patient, right payer, and right service line.*

Who is the "right patient"?

Let's assume you understand how to do the basic marketing task of target profiling. Here, *segmentation*—regardless of whether you are using a sophisticated CRM system or other research—is the first step to a successful program. Segmentation is defined as taking the whole population you serve and dividing it into small, targetable groups that are defined by similar characteristics.

The illustrations here are an example of profiles we have used to represent segmented targets. We call these two people Bob and Mary—and unfortunately, one or both of them will have an unexpected heart attack this year.

Just as the FBI develops a specific profile of a likely perpetrator when tracking an unknown suspect, marketers must also build a profile of their targets. Here at THE HEAVYWEIGHTS, we give our profiles names and discuss what their lives are like—right down to what is probably in their wallet or purse, what they are likely doing that night, and things they may be discussing. We obsess and discuss the lifestyles and habits of our imaginary friends until they become very real to us.

You can dispassionately discuss theoretical demographic profiles, or you can look at your named and illustrated "friend" and ask, "Is this communication likely to be important to Mary? We know how she *loves* Mark Harmon on NCIS, but will this YouTube video also engage her?" That type of familiarity immediately brings everyone—marketers, doctors, administrators, etc.—into sharp focus.

Clearly defined profiles also put a stop to distracting ideas. The next time a doctor wants his picture on a billboard, asks you to sponsor his favorite organization, or pay for a banquet of some kind with marketing funds, all you have to do is ask, "How is this going to get Bob or Mary into an appointment?" This is a good way to nip bad ideas in the bud.

An additional benefit of naming your demographic target is that a name gives all stakeholders a common vocabulary. This is the best way to get the team focused on whom to target and to develop an ongoing practice of evolving insights into your "close friend." All stakeholders will have a clear visual image and understanding of the patient you are targeting. As soon as you get doctors and administrators calling your targets by name, you'll know you have succeeded.

The questions you ask to start a profile are basic:

- What geographic area are they from?
- Who is their payer?
- What procedure or service do they need?
- What is their age? What are the most common names in that age group?
- What is their household income?

- What job is he or she most likely to have?
- What action do you want them to take? How will that action lead to an admission?
- What media do they consume?
- Where do they get information?
- How do they make decisions?
- What are their key relationships (family, friends, affiliations)?
- What are their likely hobbies and activities?

Make educated guesses when you don't have hard information. Each service line will be different, and so will each procedure within a service line.

After you've done your foundational marketing research work and have established a comprehensive and evolving profile of your target, you must next understand how the buying decisions are made: how does someone go from being a consumer seeing your marketing to a patient you can admit and charge?

The phrase "buying decisions" may be misleading. First, understand that nobody goes doctor shopping in the traditional sense of the word "shopping." Secondly, nobody goes doctor shopping (much less hospital shopping) in the normal course of everyday life. If you don't have a pressing need to take care of an elective surgery or medical problem, all those brand billboard and TV spots go unnoticed. Your branding may be fabulous, but consumers don't find your advertising relevant.

So, what about referring physicians? Referring physicians don't "shop" for a place to send referrals. While referring physicians are a source of admissions, changing those referral patterns is a slow and expensive process. Doctors send referrals to specialists they know and trust. Even when primary care doctors work for a health system, they are seldom loyal to their employer as a referrer. Referral patterns don't change easily, so investing a big share of your limited resources in trying to change them makes very little financial sense.

So where can you inject your brand into the buying decision process? Start by thinking about when the targeted patient has a choice. For instance, like I mentioned before, someone in the midst of having a stroke can't choose your neurology program. Then who *can* choose?

Your ideal target should:

- Be pre-episode (asymptomatic)

- Have loose medical relationships (not seeing a doctor for the diagnosis)

Or:

- Have recently received a catastrophic diagnosis

Let me define this ideal target description a little bit further.

Pre-episode patients:

This is important enough that I made it one of the titular Nine Things (#4), so we will talk about this in more detail later. For now, you need to know that provider marketing and advertising must focus on pre-episode patients: those patients that are either not yet aware they have a serious medical problem, or have been ignoring symptoms for a while.

I first understood the importance of specific targeting when I was working with an orthopedic service line. We were hosting a knee replacement informational seminar. As a test, we sent out 5,000 invitations to a list generated by the CRM team of those likely to need a knee replacement. About 5 people showed up—less than 1 percent of 1 percent. 1/1000th of the list. Very disappointing.

Then we made a discovery: the mailings were accidentally addressed to those the CRM sorted as likely to have shoulder problems. It was still an orthopedic problem: still a similar age group, but not the same as the segmentation for knees.

So we re-sent the invitations to the proper knee list: 250 people responded. Five percent versus .01 percent. That's a 50 times greater response.

The slightly different consumer target from shoulders to knees seemed like a small thing, but it made a huge difference. Remember that small changes can have huge consequences when you strategize about "where you will play."

Why? Because after a patient has a medical episode, or has pronounced symptoms that drive him or her to a doctor, that patient seldom makes any more provider choices. After an episode, the doctors and facilities are chosen and patients almost never change doctors. No one with a known cardiovascular problem would drive by your "Rated #1" billboard and decide they might need to change their cardiologist. You have to find them *before* they need a cardiologist— that is, before they have some type of episode.

Loose medical relationships:

Almost everyone says they have a doctor, but few have actually seen their doctor recently. When a patient is not under active care from a physician, we call that a *loose medical relationship*.

Statistics abound saying that if a potential problem is detected at a risk assessment event, a patient who hasn't seen their doctor within the last two years is more than 90% likely to go see the doctor you recommend. Even patients who have seen their doctor recently are more than 60% likely to make an appointment with whomever you recommend. Once they opt-in to an appointment in your system, they are no longer in a "loose relationship" and are unlikely to change doctors.

Let me sum up these last two points: when you find a problem for an asymptomatic consumer at a risk assessment, *and* they have a loose medical relationship, you have just captured a new patient, something no amount of branding or ads can do alone. *Actual patient acquisition.*

There is one other type of patient you can capture in the buying decision process:

The catastrophic diagnosis patient:

Another type of patient that can be brought quickly and cost effectively into the system is the patient that just received a *catastrophic diagnosis.*

A catastrophic diagnosis patient is someone that has just received a complicated diagnosis—for example, a malignant tumor that needs all three kinds of cancer treatments (surgery, chemotherapy, and radiation)—and has to make choices about their treatment. This is where you need a great digital strategy, because the family of someone with a complicated diagnosis will search for answers online.

Here is a hypothetical example. If, God forbid, I get a complicated brain tumor—say, a glioblastoma—I can guarantee that my wife, our friends, our family, and I will know everything there is to know about that type of tumor within the next 72 hours. We'll find out about the latest research, clinical trials, everyone who specializes in surgery, radiation therapy, and medical oncology in the country—especially in the city where we live. We will immediately get online and become experts in that type of tumor.

This is what everyone with a complicated or catastrophic diagnosis does. By *complicated*, I mean the diagnosed problem is *low incidence*. That means few people have the problem and few doctors have experience treating it. By *catastrophic*, I mean that the problem is life threatening. So, people in these situations go online to find the information they need to evaluate what to do next. That's why over half of open craniotomies (DRG 001) are performed by the neurosurgeon who gave the second (or third, or fourth, etc.) opinion.

If you have a great online program, the patient will find and evaluate your service line and doctors. I hate to sound crass by mentioning this, but any catastrophic remedy is likely to be a well-paying DRG. There is money in big, complicated problems.

Let's go back to the CEO we mentioned in the beginning of this chapter who said, "Bring the *right patient*, with the *right payer*, to the *right service line*." I have been outlining a definition of the "right patient"; now, let's move to the other two parts of this: the "right payer" and the "right service line."

Who is the "right payer"?

Mostly, but not always, this generally means a patient with a private payer. Procedures, surgeries, imaging, and a few other things can be decent Medicare/Medicaid payers, too. Mostly, however, we are targeting those with good private employer insurance.

What is the "right service line"?

When we say "right service line," we really mean a DRG/CPT at the four-way intersection of capacity, profitability, high incidence, and expertise. This is so important that it is actually one of the Nine Steps (Step #3), so we will later discuss how important it is to only use precious marketing resources to drive business where you make money and have capacity.

Look at one of your current service line ads: does it comply with all four prerequisites? Do you have the capacity to take in lots of new patients in this service line? Are you making your bottom line contribution margin on this work? Is it high-incidence—are there lots of people who could use your help? Is this an area of clinical expertise? This is a great way to quickly check the potential effectiveness of your service line communications.

I want to mention again: I am saying "service line," but what I should really be saying is "DRG/CPT." For example, don't just run general ads for your heart program: instead, decide what DRGs you want to drive in the CV service line and target those specifically.

Conclusion

So that's the first of the nine things you have to do to drive measurable and profitable patient volume. The following chapters are a lot shorter, but I felt compelled to explain the first thing in more detail than the rest — because if you don't get this right, none of the other eight things will work. Successful healthcare marketing programs start with correctly targeting a specific patient.

Step #2

COLLABORATE WITH FINANCE TO SET MEASURABLE GOALS

There is much talk in clinical healthcare about Evidence-Based Decision Making—and just like the clinical side, a key to marketing success and job security in the marketing department is *Evidence-Based Marketing*. What's hot for clinicians should be even hotter for marketing departments: making evidence-based decisions.

Not to make an obvious statement, but to make evidence-based decisions, you first have to have a way to gather evidence. In a hospital or health system, that evidence is usually related to or directly controlled by someone in finance.

Why finance? Because the value you can provide to a healthcare organization as a marketer is driving bottom line *contribution margin*. To put that in consumer marketing terms, you drive sales of the profitable services. Finance knows which services are profitable and have capacity, and they can track admissions data to give you metrics to evaluate how you are doing.

In the consumer world of non-provider-related marketing, marketing departments are required to develop revenue models. They spend a given amount of money in the hopes of turning a given amount of profit. They model different media and do A/B message testing to make the revenue model "scalable": when they spend more money, the profit they turn increases proportionately.

In provider healthcare, we usually measure using admissions data and the year-over-year number of equivalent procedures. To come up with a viable way to do that, you will need the help and cooperation of the finance team. This collaboration is essential to getting usable metric information and targeting the right DRGs/CPTs.

There is another key reason you should collaborate with finance: *your goals as a marketer and their goals as a finance team are aligned.* They want the same thing you want: to drive high-contribution patient volume into the system.

There is an old healthcare cliché that *CFOs manage to the bond rating.* But what does *managing to the bond rating* mean?

When a rating service like Moody's or Standard and Poor's evaluates the creditworthiness of a health system, they look at:

- Number of days' cash on hand
- Operating margin
- Amount of outstanding debt per bed and peak debt
- Market share and competition
- Occupancy rates
- Payer mix

Healthcare marketers drive *the right patient with the right payer to the right service line.* Therefore, they directly influence five out of the six items above—the only thing they can't change is debt. Everything apart from that can be directly influenced by an effective marketing program.

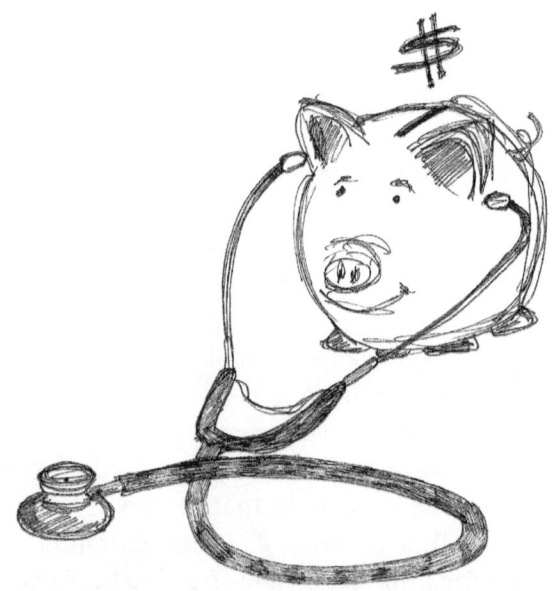

Cash on hand comes from driving contribution-rich procedures. *Operating margin* also increases when you target contribution-rich DRGs/CPTs. *Market share* changes when you expand the market for your services and become the provider of choice. *Occupancy rates* are a direct result of increased patient volume. *Payer mix* comes from consumer segmentation and targeting. You could probably even make a case that debt is reduced when you drive more cash into the system.

How do you get started with the finance team in order to use evidence-based decisions in marketing?

- Clearly define the objectives *before* you design a campaign
- Agree with the finance team about what data will be gathered and how it will be evaluated
- Set expectations that all information will be used to review and revise marketing plans—this information is used for *Continuous Process Improvement*

I should say something about that third bullet point: *Continuous Process Improvement.* You must be willing to make mistakes. You must be willing to drive little-to-no volume on your first couple of tries. But you also must review and revise your marketing based on the metrics you are gathering. An honest review of results is critically important.

Another common impediment to working with the finance team is that marketers sometimes get no credit from the finance team for admission of a patient who has been active in the system previously. For example, if the admissions data says the patient has already been treated in the hospital for diabetes, then they don't count when they become a CV patient as a result of your marketing program.

Finance people want *real* numbers. When that previous patient gets a new procedure, you can help clarify the effectiveness of your marketing if you know how they accessed the system. Did the patient attend a risk assessment, opt-in to an online survey, or get direct mail from you at their home? If so, your marketing probably drove them in. But if they were referred by the same primary care doctor who referred them for a previous diagnosis, it probably wasn't an admission caused by your marketing. Just like you, the finance team wants the truth. Work with them to dig it out so that you can make your marketing more effective.

Build a collaborative evidence-gathering system and you will reap the rewards of continuously improving results. This is good for both the financial sustainability of the health system and the job security of hospital marketers.

Step #3

CHOOSE YOUR DRGS WISELY

A hospital CEO once challenged me: "So what if marketing gets me an extra $100 million in business? It only contributes about $2 million more to the bottom line. That's not much difference when I consider the cost." We responded by demonstrating how carefully targeting the DRGs in which that $100 million comes into the hospital could turn $2 million in profits to something more like $40 million.

When I visit new health system clients for the first time, I often see their billboards on my ride from the airport advertising their service line programs. So, for instance, if they're advertising their cancer program, I ask, "Do you have excess oncology capacity? I saw lots of outdoor ads on the ride here." Many times they say, "No! We are out of beds and we don't have enough doctors, but we have a world-class program—the best in the region—and we want to tell the world about it."

I get that they have a great program and are proud of it. But it makes no business sense to spend your precious few marketing dollars on a service line into which you can't take more patients. Marketing money should only be used to drive patient volume where needed. It won't pay for itself unless you have capacity to take new patients.

We can see which DRGs to promote and how to promote them using the Capacity-Profitability Matrix. On the x-axis, graph your capacity to admit more patients. On the y-axis, chart the profitability of a DRG.

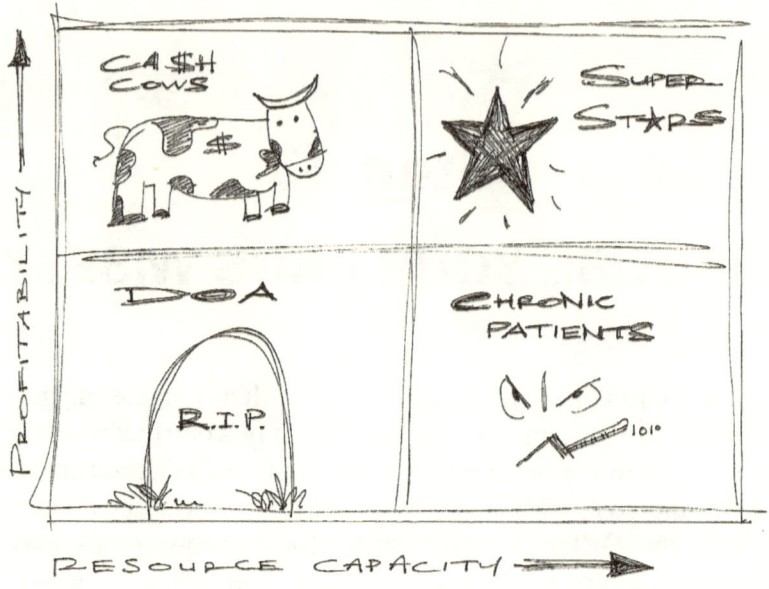

Superstars:

High-profitability DRGs that have ample staff and facilities to accommodate growth are called *Superstars*. These are aggressively promoted using the full array of marketing tools, such as broadcast, interactive, social media, highly targeted mail/direct response, physician referral programs, screenings and events, and more.

Cash Cows:

High-profitability DRGs that are at their maximum capacity are called *Cash Cows*. By *maximum capacity,* I mean that the organization doesn't have the doctors or resources to see additional patients. An example of that for some hospitals is neurosurgery: they have a neurosurgeon, but he is working as hard as possible while they have been unable to hire a second neurosurgeon to help take call and do surgeries. In a case like that, you would not spend money to promote the program. These are supported by moderate marketing efforts such as physician referral programs, targeted screenings/events, and highly targeted mail/direct response.

Chronic Patients:

Low-profitability DRGs that have an abundance of resources are called *Chronic Patients*. With operational changes, you can transfer some resources from here into the Cash Cows and Superstars. It's a delicate balance, but with a little strategic effort, you can give a boost to your profitable DRGs without sacrificing patient care.

DOA Programs:

The low-profitability, low-capacity service lines are called *DOA*. Don't waste any of your limited energy and resources here.

Marketing programs can and should always be extremely targeted. There is no case study in the country that can show a significant change in market share because of a health system branding campaign. All communications need to be highly focused and pragmatic in their approach. The way marketing succeeds (i.e., produces ROI) is by driving high-contribution DRGs (or CPTs) in clinical areas that have capacity.

It is a cliché that doctors in successful programs want the recognition that marketing can bring. Putting doctors on billboards for programs that are already near capacity is falsely justified by saying "it keeps the doctors happy" or "it has a halo effect on the whole hospital." No matter what your rationalization, it is always a bad idea for marketers to get out of the Superstar quadrant with marketing resources.

So, back to that CEO at the beginning of this chapter who ho-hummed a marginal increase of $100 million. That particular client had lots of resources (buildings, doctors, and staff) dedicated to CV procedures. There was a high *fixed cost* in buildings and salaries. The service line administrator did a great job of managing *variable costs* for doing additional procedures. They had capacity to take new patients, high-contribution DRGs, high-incidence diagnoses to treat (so there is a large market to draw from), and a highly capable staff. Once again, this is the four-way intersection where you know there is good reason to spend money driving patients to these DRGs.

Their marketing team brought in thousands of additional procedures with highly targeted marketing of risk assessments.

They increased equivalent procedures over the course of the year by well over 800 per month. The net increase in contribution margin was over $40 million that year on a little over $100 million in additional revenue.

Why did their bottom line increase so dramatically? Because they did not add any additional fixed costs (like buildings and equipment) and they already did a great job in managing variable costs (like labor and medical devices). So the net contribution margin dropped right to the bottom line.

The next time a CEO or CFO asks what they get from their marketing investment, tell them it depends on where they invest and how they target. With a little applied logic, a 2% net contribution margin can change to a 40% net contribution margin, and marketing can change from an overhead expense to a revenue generator that shows measurable ROI.

Step #4

TARGET PRE-EPISODE PATIENTS

We discussed pre-episode—asymptomatic—patients in Step #1, but it is important enough to examine in more detail here in Step #4.

I saw a Midwestern health system in a medium-sized market bring in over 400 additional CV procedures, a significant change in year-over-year equivalent procedures, *without directly competing with other local hospitals*. They just found an additional 400 procedures that other systems didn't. In that health system's specific situation (and all providers are different), that marginal increase brought in a conservative estimate of over $3 million dollars in bottom line contribution margin.

So how did they find new patients without aggressively competing for business with the other local heart programs, all of whom were aggressively advertising and branding their programs? Did they buy physician practices, build new facilities, hire new specialists, open surgery centers, or create some other expensive gambit?

No. They made no additional capital investments in facilities and they didn't acquire any other assets. They did it by actually creating a new uncontested market—and you can too. *The uncontested market is pre-episode patients.*

When I say "uncontested," I mean that nobody is targeting with their marketing or communicating to those consumers. Most health systems spend their money competing with other health systems by going after a physician or patient who can never choose them anyway. But very few providers talk to the group that can and will choose them: the asymptomatic pre-episode patient.

Marketing departments for health systems, hospitals and practices compete in expensive and ineffective ways such as advertising and physician referral programs. Physician referral patterns change very slowly, if at all. Physicians refer to other doctors they trust, or know socially. No referring physician just stops sending business to a friend without a compelling reason. Your physician liaisons can give compelling reasons to refer to your facilities all day long, but it will never trump the embarrassment a doctor will feel by telling a friend he is no longer sending him patients.

The other group we mistakenly target with advertising are consumers who already have a doctor. We *must* be talking to them because no one else pays any attention to healthcare advertising. Most consumers never notice healthcare ads or billboards because their mental filter determines that it doesn't apply to them.

As an example, you can advertise your heart program as "Nationally Recognized" or "Rated #1" ad nauseum, but if someone doesn't have a known heart diagnosis, they will ignore your advertising as completely as they do *Barbie* ads if they don't have a 4-year-old daughter. It doesn't apply to them or engage them in any relevant way. And if they do have a known diagnosis, then they are already in the healthcare machine and they are not going to change doctors just because they saw your ad,

> *Physician Liaisons I am a big fan of physician liaison programs to drive additional business into a health system or practice. But the value is in getting more business from existing referral sources.*
>
> *Sometimes there is a false expectation that liaisons can change referral patterns by directing referrals away from other physicians and toward the practices and facilities they represent. While liaisons can't change referral patterns, they still can drive increased business. There is an old business adage: "The best place to find new business is with your existing customers." This is just as true for healthcare providers as it is for other types of businesses. A liaison program can tell your existing customers about the programs and facilities they may not be fully utilizing and may also create a level of customer service that is only possible face-to-face.*

no matter how much you brag about your hospital.

Here is a common rationalization for branding advertising for service lines: "But aren't we laying a foundation for a later decision by the consumer?" No. That same consumer won't remember your advertising later when they need to make an urgent provider choice. To use the heart program example again, when the patient has a heart attack, they don't go to the hospital that has the best branding: they go to the place the ambulance can get them to the fastest. Nobody pulls the oxygen mask off their face in the ambulance and struggles to comment through the pain and fear, "Please take me to the place that has the cool ads," or "I want to go to the place the billboard said was rated highly in three clinical areas by HealthGrades."

So let's recap these last two important points. First, referral patterns do not change significantly, no matter how compelling the case your physician liaisons present to a referring physician. Second, your consumer ads are not reaching a consumer that can consciously choose your doctor or facility.

In contrast, if a patient finds out through a risk assessment or wellness training event that he or she may have a serious medical problem, *then she can make choices.* At the moment she finds out she has a problem, she will be highly motivated to make provider choices. A wise marketing team will provide clearly defined next steps to help them manage their newly discovered health problem and a way to make appointments *on the spot*—the point of contact when a problem is discovered for the first time. This is *the* moment when the door to your health system is open to a new patient.

Back to the Midwestern health system we mentioned in the beginning of this chapter: how did they find 400 new procedures without competing with other health systems? By implementing an online and location-based early detection program that asked at-risk persons if they wanted to opt in to an in-depth exam. More than 80% of at-risk persons took them up on the offer.

Instead of competing, they *expanded* the market. They didn't talk to those patients and doctors who already had made up their mind. They found people that everyone else had ignored: the person who has no idea he or she has a problem. By most statistics, at least half of consumers who have cancer, are about to have a stroke or a heart attack, or have a serious orthopedic problem, are *not* diagnosed or in the care of a doctor.

Similar successes to the CV program we mention here have been achieved in hospitals that have used organized online and in-person risk assessments for cancers, stroke, joint, spine, and bariatric procedures, just to name some of the major high-incidence, high-contribution DRGs.

This sounds simple, but efficiently executing this program takes some planning and know how to maximize your success and ROI. Done correctly, your healthcare organization will transform its public reputation from the usual money-grubbing corporate narcissist that only brags about itself in corporate communications to a valuable community asset that is working to save lives in the community you serve.

Caring instead of bragging will bring the bottom line contribution margin money in the door faster and cheaper than traditional advertising. Your bottom line and your reputation will improve simultaneously, without any need for expensive marketing competition.

Step #5

MASTER THE THREE M'S: MEDIA MIX, MESSAGE, AND MOVEMENT

I'm probably cheating a little bit here by putting three things together in just one chapter, but this combo of M's is an essential recipe to make your marketing more effective.

The recipe, while important, is also simple: 1) use a variety of media to find your target where they are likely to hear and consider your message; 2) when the message finds them, it has to be about *them*, not how supposedly great the provider is (as mentioned earlier); and 3) then give a call to action so the target knows exactly what to do next.

I will break this simple recipe down in a little more detail.

Media Mix:

Reach your target in surprising places where they can listen. Note that I say a *mix* of media. There is a combination of multiple forms of media that will drive optimal results.

A common mistake is overreliance on a single form of media. People in larger markets invest in TV spots or broadcast ads. Smaller markets may rely too much on outdoor or newspaper ads. Instead, be imaginative about what your definition of media is. For instance, besides the usual traditional and social media, you can use events, white papers, webinars, street teams, publicity stunts, and so forth. I saw a cancer program put breast exam info on the plastic bags in the produce section of a local supermarket chain. That's non-traditional media by any definition. Get creative and then measure the results.

Another common mistake is neglecting to set up a *control group* of media. A control group is a benchmark that helps you measure changes in your metrics based on tweaks to your media mix. Once you establish the numbers you use for comparison, you can then systematically add and subtract media to track the changes in your metrics. (Remember Step #2, Collaborate with Finance to Set Measurable Goals.)

For each metric you track—number of risk assessments, phone calls, opt-ins to a database, or whatever—you must also track the mix of most effective media. *Effective* here is defined as what drives the most responses for the least cost. Of course, you could spend a fortune on various media and get lots of responses, but you want to find a maximum response from reasonable media spending. *Reasonable* is usually defined as whatever your budget is at that time. Once you prove you can drive bottom line contribution margin into the system, your budget will expand. If you start driving bottom line cash, the CFO of the organization will become your biggest fan.

Motivating Message:

Craft a message that will stir your target to action; a message that the target will be surprised and delighted to hear. So what kind of message will stir, surprise, and delight? I will tell you what kind won't: *narcissistic messages*.

I know I keep coming back to this same theme, but corporate narcissism rarely pays off. This is only surprising because it is so common in healthcare marketing: some variation of "we are the best," or "we have great doctors," "we have the latest technology," or tag lines that say something about being the biggest or best or smartest. In our efforts to assure patients that they should trust us with their lives, we become bores that keep talking about ourselves. This is a losing strategy, because like always, the key to being interesting to others is being interested in *them*.

Also, when measuring the effectiveness of your message, don't be confused by *awareness* numbers. *Awareness* of your brand is a practically useless measurement. Marketing Directors love the brand awareness metric because it is easy to achieve. They say, "I know my advertising is working because our awareness numbers have been increasing." That is so wrong on so many levels I could use a chapter just to rant on the topic. But lucky for you, dear reader, I won't. Still, let me at least point out that Osama bin Laden had very high brand awareness numbers and yet nobody wanted to buy anything from him. Awareness and *understanding the value of your brand promise* are two different things.

So if corporate narcissism and brand awareness don't create a compelling brand message, then what will engage and delight your target? *Symptom messaging*, which is something that relates to the actual patient: "If you have these symptoms, here is what you should do next," or "If you want to avoid these symptoms, do this." It should be about the patient: show that you understand (have expertise) and know what they should do next. Then they are likely to trust you to help them through the next steps.

It is no wonder that Dr. Mehmet Oz grew from a segment on Oprah to being a trusted national celebrity. He discussed patients and their health issues. He explained symptoms and how to treat them, avoid them, or live with them. Frankly, people trust Dr. Oz more than any of your doctors, no matter how much braggadocio you sling out there in your marketing. If you can find that patient-centric, interesting message, then the next step is much easier.

Movement:

Movement is simply *the next move* that the listener (or viewer or reader) should take. Sometimes you may see this called an ad's *call to action.*

Always be very specific about the next step or action you want your target to take. Maybe you want them to call a phone number, visit an event or website, or go to a retail partner to pick up more information—it doesn't matter *what*; just be very specific. This is how you measure the success of the campaign. Not by awareness (as we mentioned above), but instead by engagement.

This brings us to Step #6, Opt-In Marketing. But before we turn the page, remember this before we leave the three M's: if you don't give the target an unambiguous next step, one that's easy for them to perform, all your work is worthless. You need a recipe including all three M's: the right media mix, a compelling message that is about them and not the corporate health system, and an unambiguous next move. Without all three, none of it works.

Step #6

OPT-IN MARKETING IS NOT OPTIONAL

Traditionally, advertising and marketing were one-way transmissions of messages to consumers. We focused on measuring *frequency and reach*: how many *times* someone saw our messages, and how many *people* saw our messages. But in today's world, database analysis and the interactive way digital communities work has shown us that *conversations with* our prospective customers are much more valuable than *broadcasting to* them.

This is an example of how two parties both get what they want simultaneously: a conversation with prospective new patients will get them the accurate health-related information they seek and also help providers drive measurable business into their facilities. The way to start this consumer conversation is *Opt-In Marketing*.

Opt-In Marketing is giving a prospective patient the *option* to give you their contact information and get into a dialog with you. Sometimes, this is also referred to as *Consensual Marketing* or *Permission Marketing*.

The basic idea is to transform your marketing from a one-way message broadcast by you into an interactive two-way dialogue. An interactive model defines value by the unique and individualized way your patient (or prospective patient) defines it—not the way your doctors or marketing department define it. The organization's definintion of value is not relevant to the consumer. I have already ranted about corporate narcissism and marketing braggadocio, but letting the consumer define what they want to talk about truly benefits both parties.

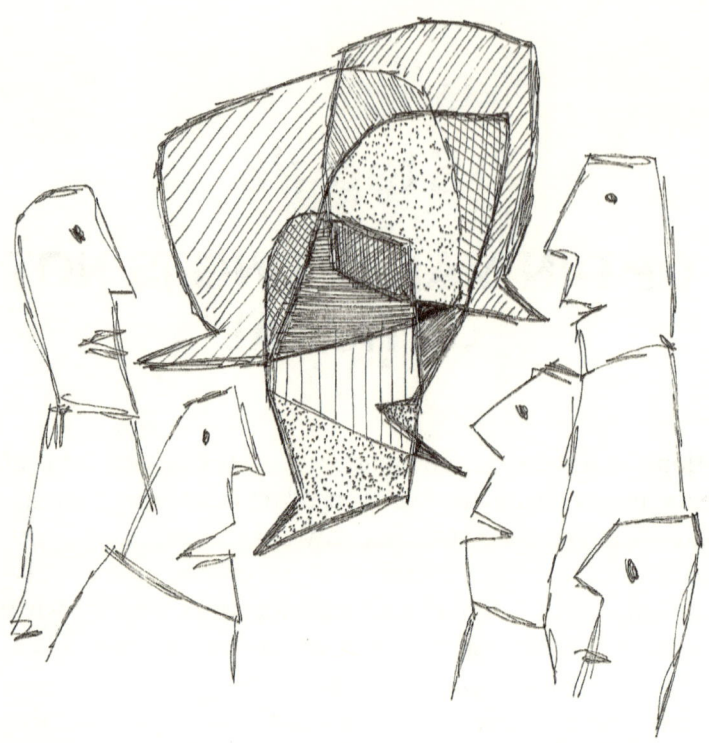

This is the very antithesis of the corporate narcissism we discussed in the "Message" part of the three Ms in the last chapter. The patient defines what she wants to talk about with you. But don't be confused. This is not just pure altruism: this will also dramatically increase ROI, and better yet, make ROI easier to measure.

Why converse online like this? The numbers are overwhelming:

- At least 67% of all prospective elective patients search the Internet before making a final provider decision (remember, for instance, that most cancer surgeries are technically elective)

- Once the patient gets into a conversation with a second opinion provider, they have an over 75% chance of selecting that provider

- Computer-based patient inquiries have a much higher probability of a great payer than telephone-based inquiries.

Okay, we get it: lots of employed people (with great payers) are online and want to us to join the conversation. So what are practical ways to entice a consumer to opt-in? Why would a consumer give you their contact information? Because you have something they want, which means they will give you their contact information in order to download something like helpful wellness information, request to talk to a nurse, register for a seminar, receive a home risk assessment kit, sign up for webinars, newsletters (or e-newsletters), or hundreds of other ideas.

So, what are your immediate next steps?

- Use patient research and CRM to understand the topics the targeted patients will likely want to discuss
- Integrate the interactive opportunities into all your advertising and messaging—make sure all messages offer an opportunity to find you online
- Redesign your web presence to optimize the patient experience, not the corporate obsessive need to communicate

(I could write another book about how horrible and unhelpful hospital websites are—ironically because they are trying to help everyone with everything at the same time)

- Collect information from online interactions to begin establishing metrics so that continuous improvement can become routine

Step #7

BECOME THE PATIENT DISTRIBUTION CZAR

The marketing department must ensure that new patients are correctly distributed to the right physicians and services. I humbly call this being the *Patient Distribution Czar.*

I use the word "czar" in a tongue-in-cheek way, but if marketing does not actively take over the job of distributing patients throughout the system, it won't get done at all. Marketing is the only job function in a position to do this.

Sorting patients offers huge benefits to both the organization and the marketing department. For the organization, getting properly diagnosed patients to the right doctor efficiently is the fastest way to build patient volume. For the marketer, you can become a better source of referrals to the specialists in your organization than the primary care doctors that you usually count on. Your relationship with doctors and others in the organization will improve as they recognize your value.

So how does this distribution process work?

Risk Assessment:

There are two ways to do risk assessment: in person and online. In both cases, the methodology is similar. In person, the risk assessment is usually administered by someone in your health promotions department or a clinical person of some type. When a patient fails a risk assessment, the person on-site should help them clarify and check their answers. If they are still at risk, move on to the next step.

When a patient fails an online risk assessment, someone on your team (at the call center, perhaps?) should call them back immediately; stats show the lead will go cold in 72 hours. This call should walk them through their answers on the risk assessment: make sure they understood the questions and put in the correct numbers. If they are still a high-risk patient after the clarification call, then go on to the next step.

Exam and Next Appointments:

Set up a face-to-face meeting with a Nurse Practitioner or an RN for a more complete (but still cursory) exam. That nurse should determine if a specialist consult is needed—or, if very severe symptoms exist, an immediate ER visit. Maybe that leg pain is an orthopedic problem and a consultation with an orthopedic surgeon is the right appointment to make next. Or maybe there are other symptoms that need to be addressed; if so, that nurse needs to be empowered to make appropriate appointments.

Everybody in the health system is now happy. You are building PC practices and specialties as appropriate. The money spent to find patients is paying off by plugging patients into the system efficiently for your physicians while truly improving patient health.

Let me give you a real-life example of what could go wrong if you skip either of these two steps. Here is a real-life example from a "successful" cardiovascular marketing program:

A campaign drove thousands of patients into risk assessments, both at events and online. Because this marketing team did a great job of segmenting the market and targeting only those who were likely to have a cardiovascular problem, the campaign drove about 20% of the total respondents who were at-risk and also asked to see a cardiologist as a next step to manage their newly discovered problem.

Impressive campaign, right? Highly effective marketing resulting in a high opt-in percentage. But if it was so successful, then why were the CV doctors so angry? How could anyone complain about bringing in hundreds of new cardiology patients?

Turns out there was a lot for the doctors to be angry about. *Just because hundreds of people failed a cardiovascular risk assessment didn't necessarily mean that they each actually had a cardiovascular problem.* The physicians' offices became overwhelmed with appointment requests, most of them from patients who didn't actually need to see a cardiologist. The system was clogged with pointless appointments.

Oops. What did we learn?

The first thing I learned from that experience is that cardiologists get upset when you clog up their appointments with people who should have seen a primary care doctor or nurse before seeing them. They get even more upset when the leg pain that caused the failure in a CV screening turns out to be an orthopedic problem.

So we go back to the two steps above. Both are equally important: you must find the at-risk patients, and then set up a face-to-face meeting with a NP or an RN who will give them a more complete (but still cursory) exam and then refer them to the right next step.

Step #8

CAPITALIZE ON CO-RISKS

Marketing to your existing patients is not only the fastest way to increase patient volume, it's also the cheapest way. Most importantly, it is the kindest thing you can do to serve your patients.

Why do I use the word "kind?" Because you have the tools that can eliminate physical suffering, possibly death and family grief, and bring vitality to the lives of those you serve.

By utilizing your CRM segmentation tools, you can identify those patients who are most at risk and help them take actions that will either prevent an episode, catch a problem earlier when treatment is likely to be less onerous and more likely to be effective, and change a self-destructive lifestyle to one of wellness and joy. That, by any definition, is a *kind* thing to do.

Many types of patients are very likely to have one or more comorbidities, meaning that the patient is likely to have more than one serious medical issue. These other risks and issues are statistically consistent enough that they are easy for a marketer to target.

For instance, I recently was allowed to review a proprietary *normative database*. "Normative" means it is set up as a benchmark of what is "normal," statistically speaking. There were some surprising discoveries in there. These are compelling examples:

- Anyone who fails a simple CV risk assessment, like a Framingham Cardiac Risk Score—whether or not it turns out that they have an actual CV problem—has a 30 percent chance of needing an orthopedic procedure, and a 10 percent chance of having cancer

- If they fail a cancer screening, the numbers are flipped: a 30 percent chance of a CV problem and 10 percent chance of an orthopedic problem

- If they are a bariatric patient, they will fail a PVD screening 97 percent of the time and have an over 30 percent chance of needing a joint replacement

- The average inpatient has a 60 percent chance of a primary or secondary diagnosis of diabetes. The list of likely co-morbidity issues is huge with diabetes, yet those patients are seldom cross-screened while being treated

- Over 80 percent of inpatients are likely to fail a sleep study and qualify for a sleep machine

Why do I assert that marketing to existing patients is the "fastest" and the "cheapest" way to drive business? There is an old adage in consumer marketing that *the best way to get new business is from your existing customers*. I previously mentioned this old adage in Step #4 when discussing physician liaisons and referral marketing to doctors, but this is also true in "consumer" marketing to existing patients.

Consumer marketers know that the cost of customer acquisition is huge: advertising, promotion, discounting, events, and anything else to attract new customers and communicate the value of their business over other competing choices. The same is true with healthcare: the best time to thoroughly investigate what other additional services you should provide a patient is when they are already engaged with you. This is just good business, and as we said at the beginning of this chapter, the *kind* thing to do. For instance, it is worth the hassle to ask your medical staff to allow in-patient cross-screenings for co-morbidity. It is the right thing to do for the health of the patient and the right thing to do for the financial health of the hospital.

So here is a rare example where healthcare provider marketing is similar to consumer marketing: your best new business comes from your existing customers.

Step #9

FOLLOW THE DOWNSTREAM REVENUE

Your successful efforts to build patient volume have a big hidden upside: *Downstream Revenue*. This later revenue will likely far exceed the amount of money generated by the initial marketing campaign.

Example #1:

A program in a medium-sized market's Academic Medical Center to increase mammograms drove in a marginal 1000+ mammograms per month for nine straight months. This was considered a fantastic success. The bottom line contribution margin (minus all costs and marketing expenses) from imaging, lab work, and biopsy surgeries was $2.7 million. There was measurable ROI. Everyone was thrilled.

But over the next year came more money from inpatient surgery, outpatient medical oncology, radiation oncology, and more imaging. The additional bottom line money a year after that nine month campaign was over $12 million. That is *in addition* to the initial $2.7 million bottom line contribution margin in the first nine months.

Example #2:

Another unexpected business driver I've seen is cardiovascular campaigns. I can't fully explain it (although I have some answers and some theories), but when a hospital runs a successful CV campaign, other procedures go up during the campaign period. Some of this gain in business is obvious from the cross-screening for other risks when a patient comes to a screening event. It happens every time. For example, a year-long CV campaign drove over $12 million additional contribution margin into the system. But the "unexplained" increase in business was over $40 million in net bottom line contribution margin.

The interesting thing about CV campaigns is that when you find a high-risk heart patient, even if they don't have an actionable cardiovascular problem, they eventually turn into a surgery patient. Not everyone that fails a CV risk assessment has a CV problem. But they are highly likely to have some kind of serious problem that needs surgical attention. CV campaigns keep paying off for years to come.

The same is true for cancer risk assessments. Joint pain seminars generate some surgeries today, but also many more over the next few years as those patients reevaluate their options and their pain worsens. Bariatric campaigns can pay off immediately, but the majority of those who get detailed information wait over three years before deciding to proceed.

The good news is that once someone has opted-in, once they are in your database, you can converse, communicate, and help them for years to come.

You are doing great work as a health system marketer. You can drive business with measurable ROI. But what you may not have noticed is the additional downstream revenue you have been driving into the system. Good marketing pays off like an annuity for years to come.

Review

My philosophy—and my consistent rant—is that if hospital marketing departments do not drive patient volume in a measurable way, they will always be just an overhead expense. But if hospital marketers deliver measurable ROI, they will be valued as a key component of long-term sustainability.

Think how much love is showered on referring physicians. But you, as a marketer, have a higher probability of driving enormous sums of money into the system. Maybe the CEO should be schmoozing you instead of them—there are certainly no federal laws against that.

Let's quickly review the Nine Things you should be doing to drive high-contribution patient volume into the health system:

Step #1: Target a Specific Patient

No general targets like "women 35–64." Every service line has a specific segment of the market they are targeting; many have several. Orthopedics, for instance, has different segmentation for joint replacement, shoulder surgery, and sports medicine. Bring the right patient, with the right payer, into the right DRG/CPT.

Step #2: Collaborate with Finance to Set Measurable Goals

The goals of the CFO and of the marketing department are closely aligned: to drive bottom line net contribution margin into the system. In order to make evidence-based marketing decisions, you need a way to gather evidence. Evidence in healthcare systems is usually related to, or directly controlled by, someone in finance. Working with the finance department allows you to clearly set goals that can be tracked and measured.

Step #3: Choose Your DRGs Wisely: The Most Profitable DRGs Where the Organization Has Excess Capacity

It makes no business sense to spend your marketing dollars where you have no growth capacity or little profitability. Where do you have both capacity and contribution margin? The place those two intersect is your sweet spot. The best sweet spot is the four-way intersection of capacity, profitability, capability (where you have great expertise), and high incidence (where a lot of people need help).

Step #4: Target Pre-Episode Patients

Don't spend your money marketing to people who can't or won't choose you. When somebody has a heart attack, for example, they're not going to choose your hospital because of your ads or branding. They're going to go to whatever hospital they can get to first. By marketing to people who *can* choose your hospital, you can bring in more money in initial and downstream revenue.

Step #5: Master the Three M's: Media Mix, Message, and Movement

1) Reach your target in surprising places where they can listen, 2) use a message that will stir them to action, and 3) give a clearly defined next move, or call to action, so they know exactly what to do next.

Step #6: Opt-In Marketing is Not Optional

Transform your marketing from a one-way message to an interactive dialogue with patients. Don't talk *at* them; give them an opportunity to ask questions. Start a conversation.

Step #7: Become the Patient Distribution Czar

The marketing department must take the initiative to make sure that the patients brought in by campaigns are sent to the proper appointments. Sending someone who has an orthopedic problem to a cardiologist upsets everyone involved and loses a valuable opportunity to both help a patient and make some bottom line contribution margin.

Step #8: Capitalize on Co-Risks

Did you know that 30% of joint replacement patients have a CV problem that needs surgery? Or over 40% of patients who fail a CV risk assessment have either an orthopedic problem or cancer? Once you find these profitable patients, sort and distribute them.

Step #9: Follow the Downstream Revenue

You set up the metrics with finance in Step #2; now track these patients through the system. Your marketing success and job security depend on it.

About the Author

John Luginbill: Marketing Strategist. Speaker. Author. Family Man.

Marketing Strategist:

As the CEO of the marketing firm THE HEAVYWEIGHTS in Indianapolis, IN, John has worked with some of America's greatest brands, including Nike, McDonald's, Walmart, and Thomas' English Muffins. John is particularly passionate about developing strategies and programs to increase patient volume and advance the mission of health systems, hospitals, FQHCs, and medical practices. Beyond strategic marketing and advertising campaigns, THE HEAVYWEIGHTS offers an array of services ranging from online education resources to social media training.

Speaker:

John is an in-demand speaker and has presented to marketing professionals, hospital systems, and social media enthusiasts across the country. His humor and uncensored honesty have made him a crowd favorite: those who hear him speak are engaged by his knowledge, enthusiasm, and light-hearted tone. If you'd like to contact John regarding a speaking engagement, webinar, or panel, you can reach him through his blog at TurnUpYourVolume.com.

Author:

An avid reader himself, John is the author of the blog TurnUpYourVolume.com, offering education and commentary to healthcare marketers looking to increase their patient volume. He is also the author of *Social Media, the New Digital Reality, and Provider Healthcare Marketing*, an exploration of the six key steps to understanding how digital marketing can help doctors save lives, lower the cost of delivering healthcare, and help them become financially sustainable.

Family Man:

Outside of work, John is a devoted husband, father, and friend. He loves spending time with his family and is passionate about justice, helping those in need, and being a constant learner.

Contact: You can contact John at THE HEAVYWEIGHTS at (317) 684-7777, via his blog at www.TurnUpYourVolume.com, or via Twitter @JohnLuginbill.

www.ingramcontent.com/pod-product-compliance
Lightning Source LLC
Chambersburg PA
CBHW021920170526
45157CB00005B/2113